"In the name of Allah,
the Compassionate, the Merciful"

ISBN 978-1438243474

Printed in the United States of America

How to Use These Books

The Mini Tafseer Book Series is designed to teach children the Tafseer (exegesis) of all the suwaar (chapters) in the 30th Part of the Qur'aan. Each book in this 38 book series covers a different surah. The books feature:

- Special facts about the surah
- Arabic text of the surah
- English transliteration (to assist non-Arabic speakers)
- English translation
- Simplified Tafseer
- Illustrations/Coloring pages (no animals/humans)
- Highlighted Arabic vocabulary
- Sahih Ahadith
- One sentence summary of what the surah is about
- Review section
- Notes on the text (additional facts and information)

Teaching Tips:

If your younger child has trouble going through the whole book in one sitting, or does not retain all of the information taught, then just focus on the Tafseer pages first (i.e. those that explain the verses of the surah) and save the additional information contained in the Quick Facts, What's Special, Asbaab An-Noozool, and Vocabulary sections* for later when your child has mastered the Tafseer.

For older or advanced students who need more of a challenge, you can take time to go through all sections and discuss the lesson notes for that section (located at the end of the text). This will make lessons more challenging and provide a deeper understanding of the Tafseer, and Allah knows best.

*Some books may not contain all of these sections.

Mini Tafseer Book Series

Suratun-Nasr

Quick Facts About Suratun-Nasr...

Suratun-Nasr was most likely revealed in **Madinah,** however, there are some scholars who say it was revealed in **Makkah,** and Allah knows best! [1]

Suratun-Nasr was the **last surah** revealed to Rasulullahﷺ.[2]

"Nasr" in Arabic means **help**, and Suratun-Nasr talks about how Allah helped Rasulullahﷺ.

Nasr is one of the smallest suwaar in the Qur'aan, it has **only 3 ayaat** (verses)!

So what is Suratun-Nasr
all about...

Suratun-Nasr is both happy and sad...

Suratun-Nasr is all about how Rasulullahﷺ peacefully triumphed over the Makkans, and spread Islaam across Arabia, **with the help of Allah.** That is the happy part.

The sad part was that Rasulullahﷺ needed to **prepare to go back to Allah** (because he was going to die soon), since his work in this world was complete.

Now let's learn what makes
Suratun-Nasr so…

The **first thing** that is so special about Suratun-Nasr is...

The reward of reading it is equal to reading one fourth of the Qur'aan![3]

The Messengerﷺ once asked a man..."Do you not have (i.e. have you not memorized) 'When the victory of Allah has come and the conquest (i.e. **Suratun-Nasr**)?'

The man replied: "Certainly!"

The Prophetﷺ then said, "It is (equivalent to) **one quarter** of the Quran."

The **second thing** that is so special about Suratun-Nasr is that...

It was the last surah revealed to Rasulullah ﷺ

When Angel Gibreel taught Rasulullahﷺ Suratun-Nasr, it was the **last complete surah** that Angel Gibreel would bring himﷺ.

Although, there were a few other ayaat that Angel Gibreel brought later to add to other suwaar that were almost finished, **no new surah** was revealed after Suratun-Nasr.

Now that we have learned
what is special about Suratun-Nasr,
let's get ready to learn
Suratun-Nasr itself...

We will start by learning **4 new words.**
The more words you know, the better
you will understand each surah that you
learn insha-Allah.

Understanding the Qur'aan is what Allah
wants us to do!

So let's get started
right now!

4 NEW WORDS!

Vocabulary List

Keep a look out for the following vocabulary words while you read! These words will help you remember the meaning of Suratun-Nasr, insha-Allah!

help	نَصْرُ (nasr)
the victory (winning)	اَلْفَتْحُ (al-futh)
religion (Islaam)	دِين (deen)
crowds (of people)	أَفْوَاجًا (af-waa-jaa)

Bonus: Can you find one of the vocabulary words that you learned in Unit 2?

Hint: It's on page 32 and you learned it in the book about Suratun-Naas!

Now that we are ready, we need
to start the right way...

There are **two things** we should say before we start reading a surah from the Qur'aan, and you will learn about these two things right now...

Color in your numbers!

#1 We say the Isti'aathah[4]...

I seek refuge with Allah from the
cursed Shaytaan.

('A-'oo-thoo-bil-laa-he-me-nash-shay-taa-nir-ra-jeem)

أَعُوذُ بِٱللّٰهِ مِنَ
ٱلشَّيْطَانِ ٱلرَّجِيمِ

We start reading Qur'aan by asking Allah to protect us from Shaytaan and...

#2 We say the Basmallah₅...

In the name of Allah, the Entirely Merciful,
the Especially Merciful.

(Bis-mil-laa-hir-rah-maa-nir-ra-heem)

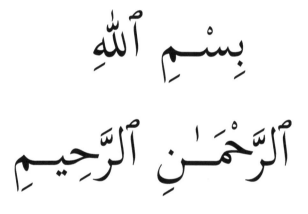

بِسْمِ ٱللّٰهِ

ٱلرَّحْمَـٰنِ ٱلرَّحِيمِ

We remember Allah and say how
great He is for giving us so many
wonderful blessings!

Okay!

We are ready to go now! You know your **new words** and you've said the **Isti'aathah** and **Basmallah**...

We will start by learning about
why and when Suratun-Nasr was
revealed!

A Story of Peaceful Triumph!

Many of the ayaat (verses) in the Qur'aan have a story behind them that tells why they were revealed. These stories are called...

Asbaab An-Noozool

The story behind the revelation of Suratun-Nasr is about how Rasulullahﷺ peacefully won Makkah, and expanded Islaam across Arabia, **with the help of Allah!**[6]

Let's start at the beginning...

Rasulullahﷺ started teaching Islaam in Makkah, but the Quraysh (the ruling tribe of Makkah) did not like it; they treated the Muslims very badly. So, Allah told the Muslims to go live in another city, called **Madinah**; there the people would welcome them. This move to Madinah is called the **"Hijrah"**.[7]

Although the Muslims found safety in Madinah, the Kaabah was in Makkah, and Allah wanted Rasulullahﷺ to make the Kaabah (and Makkah) a place for Muslims to worship only Allah.

At the same time, many of the tribes around Makkah wanted to see if Rasulullahﷺ could beat the Quraysh and make Makkah for the Muslims, too. They thought if Rasulullahﷺ could do that, he must really be sent by Allah.

At first, it did not look like the Muslims could do it. They did not have a lot of soldiers to fight. But that would change in time, **with the help of Allah**...

25

Allah helped the Muslims return to Makkah!

After being in Madinah for about **8 years**, the Muslims were finally strong enough to come back to Makkah. Allah had helped the Muslims win important battles, and now their army numbered **more than 10,000 men.**

When Rasulullahﷺ and his army arrived in Makkah, the Quraysh did not fight back at all. Allah helped the Muslims by putting fear in the hearts of the Makkans, so that they hid in their houses or stayed at the Kabah for protection.

Rasulullahﷺ told the Quraysh that **they would be safe** as long as they stayed inside and did not come out to fight. Then he ordered his men to clean out all the idols from the Kabah. This great victory is called **"Fut-hoo Makkah",** or The Conquest of Makkah.[8]

The Kabah[9] and Makkah had been won for the Muslims, and now even more things were about to change **with the help of Allah...**

27

Allah helped the Muslims win all of Arabia!

Once Rasulullah got back to Madinah,[13] people started spreading the news that the Muslims had beaten the Quraysh and won Makkah for the Muslims.

Then **large delegations** (that means groups of people representing their tribes) came from all over Arabia to say that they would be Muslims, too! [14]

It was because of this **amazing triumph** (i.e. winning Makkah and converting the tribes to Islaam peacefully) that Suratun-Nasr was revealed. [15]

Now let's learn what Suratun-Nasr says...

First, Allah told Rasulullah ﷺ
to look for <u>two signs</u>...

"When comes the Help of Allah, and Victory,"

(Ee-thaa jaaa-a nas-rool-laa-hee wal-fut)

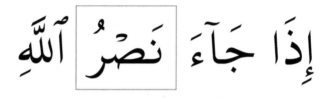

Allah told Rasulullah ﷺ...

The Muslims would win a
big battle with the **help** of Allah! **16**

This battle was "Fut-hoo Makkah",
that we talked about before.

This was the first sign...

"And you see the people entering the religion of
Allah (Islaam) in crowds,"

(Wa-ra-ay-tan-naa-sa yad-khoo-loo-na fee
dee-nil-laa-hee af-waa-jaa)

وَرَأَيْتَ ٱلنَّاسَ

يَدْخُلُونَ فِى دِينِ

ٱللَّهِ أَفْوَاجًا ۝

Then Allah told Rasulullah ﷺ...

People will become Muslims in
BIG GROUPS. [17]

This happened when Rasulullah ﷺ
returned to Madinah. We talked about
that before, too.

This was the second sign...

After Rasulullah ﷺ
saw the two signs...

...what was he
supposed to do?

"Celebrate the praises of your Lord, and pray for His Forgiveness:
For He is Oft-Returning (in Grace and Mercy)."

(Fa-sab-bih bee-ham-dee rab-bee-ka was-tagh-fir
in-na-hoo kaa-na tow-waa-baa)

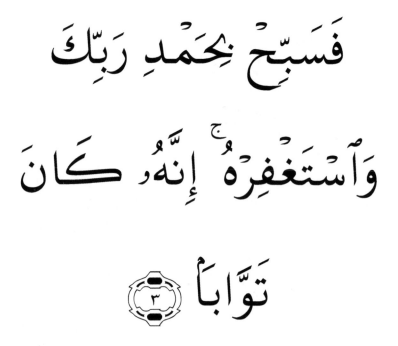

فَسَبِّحْ بِحَمْدِ رَبِّكَ

وَٱسْتَغْفِرْهُ إِنَّهُ كَانَ

تَوَّابًا ﴿٣﴾

Allah told Rasulullah ﷺ to thank Him for all of His blessings and to ask for forgiveness.

Rasulullah ﷺ did exactly what Allah told him to do. He started to praise Allah and ask for forgiveness day and night.

He praised Allah, and asked for forgiveness so often, that his wife, Aishah رضي الله عنها, asked him why he was saying it so much? Rasulullah ﷺ told her that he was doing it because Allah told him to in Suratun-Nasr. [18]

Rasulullah ﷺ knew why Allah had asked him to do this. It was because his work as a prophet was done, and now he was going to die and go back to Allah.

Death was coming, and Rasulullah ﷺ wanted to be ready to meet Allah.

Do you think Rasulullahﷺ was sad that he was going to die?

No, Rasulullahﷺ was not sad.

Rasulullahﷺ knew he had finished his work and now there were **many, many Muslims**.

He knew that after he died he would be with all of the other prophets in Jannah.

For Rasulullahﷺ, this life had been very difficult, and the work he had done had been hard, **so going back to Allah would be a relief**.

Do you think Rasulullah's ﷺ family and friends were sad to hear that he was going to die?

Yes, they were sad, but they knew that Rasulullah ﷺ had done his job.

They knew that all men die, and Rasulullah ﷺ must die at some time, too.

They knew that **Allah does not die**, and what Rasulullah ﷺ had taught them would never die either.

Last Illness of Rasulullah ﷺ...[19]

It was less than **one year**[20] after Suratun-Nasr was revealed that Rasulullahﷺ became **very ill**.

During this illness, Rasulullahﷺ was not able to walk by himself, yet he still had the Sahaabah take him to each of his wives' homes so that he could visit each one on her assigned day.

However, it was hard on him, in his heart he wished to stay in his wife **Aishah's** ﵂ home, as it was there that he was most comfortable. He did not want to make his other wives feel bad, so he would ask each day **'Where will I be tomorrow?'** so that he would know when he would be back in Aishah's ﵂ home again.

His wives understood what he wanted and had mercy on him; they gave him permission to stay with Aishah ﵂ so that he would not have to keep moving from house to house.

An example of the type of homes people lived in at the time of Rasulullahﷺ.

The Illness Worsens...

Even though Rasulullahﷺ was now more comfortable and able to rest, his illness became worse, so much so that Rasulullahﷺ could not even go out and lead the people in salaah at the Masjid (he prayed at home instead).

Salaah time would come and Rasulullahﷺ would ask for water to make wudu', but each time they would bring it, he would fall unconscious and would not be able to go.

So, Rasulullahﷺ told Abu Bakr رضي الله, his friend, to lead the people instead. This went on for several days until one Monday morning, while Abu Bakr رضي الله was leading the people in Fajr prayer, the people saw Rasulullahﷺ lift the curtain to Aishah's رضي الله house so that he could look and see them.

They thought he might come to lead the salaah, but he was too weak. He indicated for them to continue the prayer and smiled at them. **This was the last time that any of them saw Rasulullahﷺ before his death.**

An example of a water jug and basin that people might have used at the time of Rasulullahﷺ.

Death of Rasulullahﷺ...

Rasulullahﷺ died that day, before the time for Salaatul-Dhuhur, while resting his head on Aishah's رضي الله lap.

She had just brushed his teeth with a **siwaak** (wooden toothbrush), and his last words were...

"With those on whom You have bestowed Your grace, with the prophets and the truthful ones, the martyrs and the good doers. Oh Allah, forgive me and have mercy upon me and join me to the companionship on high."

At first, the people did not want to believe that Rasulullahﷺ had died. They began to gather at the masjid and argue. Umar رضي الله even threatened to kill anyone who said Rasulullahﷺ had died (this was because of the terrible sadness he felt in his heart).

But then Abu Bakr رضي الله came and reminded everyone that Rasulullahﷺ was a man, and **all men must die**. Although the Sahaabah were sad, they knew that he was right.

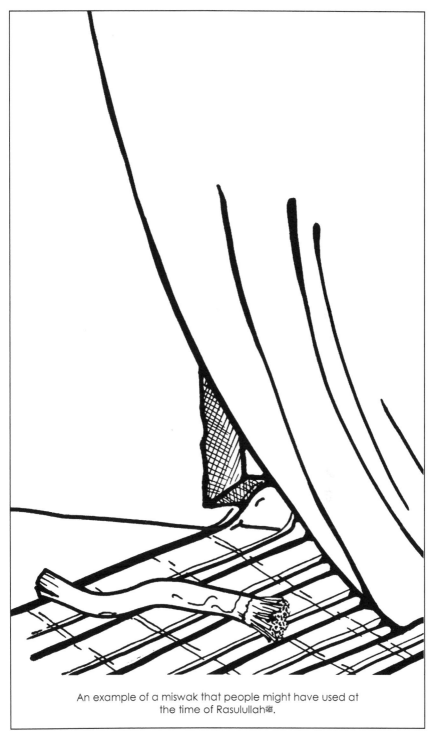

An example of a miswak that people might have used at
the time of Rasulullah.

Burial of Rasulullah ﷺ...

The Sahaabah listened to Abu Bakr رضي الله عنه and prepared to bury Rasulullah ﷺ.

They dug Rasulullah's ﷺ grave inside of Aishah's رضي الله عنها house in the exact spot where he had died, because Rasulullah ﷺ had said prophets die at the spot where they are supposed to be buried.

Rasulullah's ﷺ body was washed the next day by his cousin, Ali رضي الله عنه, with the help of several other men from Rasulullah's ﷺ family.

Rasulullah's ﷺ body was wrapped in three white sheets, the Janazah (funeral) prayer was said, and he was finally buried late in the night. This was the time that Rasulullah ﷺ had been waiting for, **ever since the day that Allah revealed Suratun-Nasr to him.**

Till this day we can go to visit Rasulullah's grave, and give him salaams if we travel to **Masjid An-Nabawi** in Madinah, Saudi Arabia.

Masjid An-Nabawi as it appears to today. The green dome (over Rasulullah'sﷺ grave) and the surrounding minarets were added during various stages of expansion and renovation after the prophet'sﷺ time.

So, what is Suratun-Nasr about?

Suratun-Nasr told Rasulullahﷺ to look for **two signs of Allah's help**...

1. The Muslims would win a **great victory**.
2. People would come in **large groups** to accept Islaam.

When he saw these signs, it would mean his work was done. Then he would need to get ready to go back to Allah, by praising Allah and asking forgiveness as much as possible.

Rasulullahﷺ knew that after these two things happened **he would die**... and he did; may Allah's peace and blessings be upon him.

The End.

Suratun-Nasr Review

Where was Suratun-Nasr revealed?

Suratun-Nasr was most likely revealed in Madinah, however, there are some scholars who say it was revealed in Makkah, and Allah knows best.

What is so special about Suratun-Nasr?

Suratun-Nasr was the last complete surah revealed to Rasulullahﷺ.

What is the Asbaab An-Noozool of Suratun-Nasr revealed?

Allah granted the Muslims a great victory in Fut-hoo Makkah (The Conquest of Makkah).

Afterwards delegations came from all over Arabia to become Muslims. It was at this time that Suratun-Nasr was revealed to inform Rasulullahﷺ of the completion of his mission and his death.

What did Allah tell Rasulullahﷺ in Suratun-Nasr?

Allah told Rasulullahﷺ to look for two signs.

What was the first sign?

The Muslims would have a great victory with the help of Allah.

What was the second sign?

People would become Muslims in big groups.

What was Rasulullahﷺ told to do when he saw the signs?

He was to praise Allah and ask for forgiveness as much as possible.

Why was heﷺ supposed to praise Allah and ask for forgiveness?

He was supposed to praise Allah ask for forgiveness in order to get ready for his death.

Did Rasulullah see the two signs Allah told him to look for?

Yes, the great victory was Fut-hoo Makkah, and the groups of people entering Islaam was the delegations from the tribes around Makkah.

 Why didn't the Muslims have to fight the Quraysh during Fut-hoo Makkah?

Allah put fear in the hearts of the Quraysh and they hid in their homes or at the Kabah to avoid fighting the Muslims.

 Why did the people around Makkah become Muslim after the Conquest of Makkah?

They thought Rasulullah must be a prophet if he could take over Makkah from the powerful Quraysh.

 What did Suratun-Nasr tell Rasulullah about himself?

It informed him that he would die soon.

Did Rasulullah ﷺ die after Suratun-Nasr was revealed?

Yes, less than a year later.

 What did Rasulullah ﷺ die from?

He had an illness that made him unable to walk and in which he often became unconscious.[21]

 Where did Rasulullah ﷺ die?

In Aishah's ﵁ home.

 Who was with Rasulullah ﷺ when he died?

His wife Aishah ﵁.

 What were the last things Rasulullah ﷺ did?

He brushed his teeth with a siwaak and made du'a to Allah while he was laying his head on Aishah's ﵁ lap.

 Where was Rasulullah ﷺ buried?

Where he died; in Aishah's ﵁ house.

Who washed Rasulullah's ﷺ body?

Ali ﷺ, his cousin, did it with the assistance of some of Rasulullah's ﷺ male relatives.

What was Rasulullah ﷺ buried in?

Three white sheets.

Can we visit Rasulullah's ﷺ grave today?

Yes, it is located under the green dome at Masjid An-Nabawi in Madinah, Saudi Arabia.

Notes to the text

[1] There is some difference of opinion about the exact time when this surah was revealed. Ibn Kathir is of the opinion that this surah was revealed in Madinah, but notes that some scholars believe it was revealed in Makkah. There also is a third opinion that it was revealed in Mina during the Farewell Pilgrimage. All versions have ahadith support their view.

What we do know for sure is that it was definitely after the Hijrah, and close to the time of the Prophet'sﷺ death, but there are various opinions as to when and where. We have opted to use the earliest evidence of revelation as recorded in the Tafseer of Ibn Kathir and Asbaab An-Nuzul of Al-Wahidi, and Allah knows best. This version holds that Nasr was revealed after the Conquest of Makkah and Battle of Hunayn (which happened within four weeks of each other). These events took place approximately one to two years before the Prophet'sﷺ death.

The explanation for the difference of opinion may be that the particular Sahaabah relating each hadith heard of this surah at the time thinking it was the time of revelation, when in fact the surah had already been revealed at an earlier time (but they were unaware of this) and Allah knows best.

2 Abdullah bin Abbas رضي الله عنه reported that this (Suratun-Nasr) is the last Surah of the Quran to be revealed, i. e. no complete surah was sent down to Rasulullah ﷺ after it.
(Sahih Muslim)

There is some dispute over what are the last verses of the Qur'aan revealed some say Suratun-Nasr, others say Maaidah 5:4. However, there is no dispute that Nasr was the last **complete surah** revealed while Maaidah was a final addition to a surah that had been almost completely revealed already, and Allah knows best.

It must be noted, that although Suratun-Nasr is the last surah to be revealed, it is not the last surah in the Qur'aan according to order. Rather Suratun-Naas is the last surah (#114) in the Qur'aan.

To explain, the order in which the Qur'aan was revealed was linked to specific events in time so that the people would understand the verses in context and could pass this information on to later generations. Once all the verses of the Qur'aan were revealed, Angel Gibreel read the entire Qur'aan, with the surahs in the order we know today, from beginning to end with Rasulullah ﷺ twice during Ramadaan in the year of Rasulullah's ﷺ death.

The Qur'aan we have today was written down based on this order from the memories and written records of the Sahaabah after the death of Rasulullahﷺ.

[3] Imaam At-Tirmidhi related from Anaas Ibn Maalik that the Messengerﷺ once asked a man, "Are you married?" He replied, "No, I swear by Allah, O Messenger of Allah! For I have nothing, so how can I marry?" Heﷺ asked the man, "Do you not have 'Say: `He is Allah, the One.' (i.e. Suratul-Ikhlaas)?" The man replied, "Certainly!" Heﷺ said: "It is (equivalent to) one third of the Quran." Then heﷺ asked, "Do you not have 'When the victory of Allah has come and the conquest' (i.e. **Suratun-Nasr**)?" The man replied, "Certainly!" The Prophetﷺ then said, "It is (equivalent to) **one quarter** of the Quran."

[4] Allah has said that we should seek refuge with Him from Shaytaan before reciting Qur'aan by saying, "A-oo-thoo-bill-laa-he-min-nash-shay-taan-nir-ra-jeem".

(So when you) want to recite the Qur'an, seek refuge with Allah from Shaytaan, the outcast (the cursed one). (Qur'aan 16:98).

The majority of scholars state that reciting this phrase, known as the Isti'aathah in Arabic (pronounced Is-ti-`aa-thah), is recommended and not required, and therefore, not reciting it

does not constitute a sin. However, Rasulullah☰ always said the Isti`aathah. In addition, the Isti`aathah wards off the evil of Shaytaan, which is necessary; the rule is that the means needed to implement a requirement of the religion is itself also required. And when one says, "I seek refuge with Allah from the cursed devil." Then this will suffice.
(Tafseer Ibn Kathir)

5 Saying the Basmallah, "Bis-mil-laa-hir-rah-maa-nir-ra-heem" before reciting any surah, except for the ninth, Suratut-Towba, which does not have the Basmallah in the beginning, is agreed upon by all scholars past and present.

6 "(When Allah's succor and the triumph cometh...) [110:1-3]. This was revealed when the Prophet☰ left from the Battle of Hunayn (author's note: four weeks after Fut-hool-Makkah, on the way back to Madinah). The Prophet☰, lived only two years after this battle (authors note: some reports say one year, Allah knows best). Ibn Abbaas ﷺ who said: "When the Messenger of Allah☰, returned from the Battle of Hunayn and Allah, exalted is He, revealed (When Allah's succor and the triumph cometh), he☰ said: 'O Ali ibn Abi Talib! O Fatimah! Allah's succor and triumph has come, I have seen people entering the religion of Allah in troops, I therefore hymn the praises of my Lord and seek forgiveness of Him, for He is ever ready to show mercy'."
(Asbab An-Nuzul by Al-Wahidi)

Ibn Abbaas رضي الله said, "Umar رضي الله used to bring me into the gatherings with the old men of (the battle of) Badr. However, it was as if one of them felt something in himself (against my attending). So he said, `Why do you (Umar رضي الله) bring this (youth) to sit with us when we have children like him (i.e. his age)' So Umar رضي الله replied, `Verily, he is among those whom you know. Then one day he called them and invited me to sit with them, and I do not think that he invited me to be among them that day except to show them. So he said, `What do you say about Allah's statement, (When there comes the help of Allah and the Conquest.)' Some of them said, `We were commanded to praise Allah and seek His forgiveness when He helps us and gives us victory.' Some of them remained silent and did not say anything. Then he (Umar رضي الله) said to me, `Is this what you say, O Ibn Abbaas رضي الله ?' I said, `No.' He then said, `What do you say' I said, `It was the end of the life of Allah's Messengerﷺ that Allah was informing him of. Allah said, (When there comes the help of Allah and the Conquest.) which means, that is a sign of the end of your life. (So, glorify the praises of your Lord, and ask His forgiveness. Verily, He is the One Who accepts the repentance and Who forgives.)' So, `Umar bin Al-Khattab رضي الله said, `I do not know anything about it other than what you have said."
(Sahih Bukhari)

7 There is some difference of opinion about the exact dates of the Hijrah, as well as the number of days that it took, however according to the most reliable reports, it most likely occurred from Safar 27 1A.H., till the 12th of Rabi' Al-Awwal 1A.H. (Ar-Raheeq Al-Makhtum, p. 168-177). This was in the fourteenth year of prophethood. It is from this year that the Muslim calendar dates.

8 Fut-hoo Makkah occurred in Ramadaan 8 A.H.

9 The illustration of the Kabah included in the text may look unusual to some due to the lack of the arches and minarets surrounding the Kabah, and the covering differing from the well known black silk cover with golden embroidery.

To explain, the Kabah has not always looked the way that we are familiar with today. The covering of the Kabah, known as the Kiswah, predates Islaam. The Kiswah originally was not black, but done in various colors. It was only later, after the death of Rasulullahﷺ (some say during the later Caliphates), that the cover was changed to black.

As for the structure surrounding the Kabah, known as the Haram, this was built in stages starting from the time of Umarرضي الله عنه. It was during his Caliphate that the first short wall was built around the Kabah to form a prayer area to accommodate more worshippers. Further expansion took place at various intervals throughout history that resulted in the massive Haram structure that we see today.

Therefore, in order to more closely approximate what the Kabah might have looked like at the time of Rasulullahﷺ, we have depicted the Kabah with a Kiswah that is colored, not black or embroidered, and without the surrounding Haram, and Allah knows best.

[10] Summarized from Ar-Raheeq Al-Makhtum, p. 403-416.

[11] Although Makkah was Rasulullah'sﷺ birthplace, the Qiblah (direction of prayer) and the holiest city, the Prophet ﷺ preferred to make Madinah his home (and rule the Islamic nation from there as well) because of the great kindness of the Ansaar (people of Madinah, known as 'helpers'). The Ansaar had welcomed the Muslims to their city when they (the Muslims) were weak and oppressed by the Quraysh.

[12] *"Assuredly Allah did help you in many battle-fields and on the Day of Hunayn: Behold! your great numbers elated you, but they availed you naught: the land, for all that it is wide, did constrain you, and ye turned back in retreat. But Allah did pour His calm on the Messenger and on the believers, and sent down forces which ye saw not: He punished the unbelievers; thus doth He reward those without Faith."*
(Qur'aan 9:25-26)

13 Rasulullahﷺ did not go directly to Madinah after the Battle of Hunayn, but rather chased the Hawazin and Banu Thaqif to Ta'if where they had a fortress. The Muslims besieged the fortress for 10-20 days, but were unable to breach it. Facing the possibility of a drawn-out fight, and with dwindling supplies, Rasulullahﷺ decided to call of the siege and return to Madinah.
(Ar-Raheeq Al-Makhtum, p. 409)

14 Amr bin Salamah ﷻ said, "When Makkah was conquered, all of the people rushed to the Messenger of Allahﷺ to profess their Islaam. The various regions were delaying their acceptance of Islam until Makkah was conquered. The people used to say, `Leave him and his people alone. If he is victorious over them he is a (true) Prophet.'"
(Sahih Al-Bukhari)

15 See note 6.

16 "The meaning of Al-Fath here is the conquest of Makkah, and there is only one view concerning it. For indeed the different areas of the Arabs were waiting for the conquest of Makkah before they would accept Islam. They said, "If he (Muhammad is victorious over his people, then he is a (true) Prophet." So when Allah gave him victory over Makkah, they entered into the religion of Allah (Islam) in crowds. Thus, two years did not pass (after the conquest of Makkah) before the peninsula of

the Arabs was laden with faith. And there did
not remain any of the tribes of the Arabs except
that they professed (their acceptance) of Islam.
And all praise and blessings are due to Allah."
(Tafseer Ibn Kathir)

17 See note 16.

18 Aishah ﷛ said, "The Holy Messengerﷺ often used
to recite *Subhanak-Allahumma wa bi-hamdika
astaghfiruka wa atubu ilaika* (according to some
other traditions, *Subhan Allahi wa bi hamdi-hi as-
taghfirullaha wa atubu ilaihi*) before his death. I
asked, "O Messenger of Allah, what are these
words that you have started reciting now?" Heﷺ
replied, "A sign has been appointed for me so that
when I see it, I should recite these words, and it is:
Idha jaa nasrullahi wal-fath."
(Sahih Muslim)

 In other traditions on the same subject Aishah ﷛
has reported that the Holy Prophetﷺ often recited
the following words in his ruku and sajdah:
*Subhanak-Allahumma wa-bi hamdika,
Allahumma- aghfirli*. This was the interpretation of
the Quran (i. e. of Surah An-Nasr) that he had
made.
(Sahih Al-Bukhari and Sahih Muslim)

19 The story of Rasulullah'sﷺ last illness, death
and burial have been summarized from the
well-known biography of the prophetﷺ,
Ar-Raheeq Al-Makhtum, p. 471-482.

Please note that all illustrations in this section (with the exception of the image of the current day Masjid An-Nabawi) represent approximate reconstructions of the items, furnishings, and construction methods that were commonly found in homes at the time of Rasulullahﷺ and are not intended to depict an exact recreation of the prophet's home at the time of his death, and Allah knows best.

The image of Masjid An-Nabawi depicts how it looks today. The masjid did not look like this at the time of Rasulullahﷺ.

20 There is a difference of opinion as to the exact amount of time that passed from the revelation of Suratun-Nasr until the death of Rasulullahﷺ. The reports range from 1 year to slightly more than 2 years, and Allah knows best. We have opted to use 1 year as the timeframe as this is the opinion of Ibn Kathir.

21 The exact nature of the illness Rasulullahﷺ suffered from is not known. However, it is recorded in Sahih ahadith that Rasulullahﷺ mentioned that he was feeling the after effects of being poisoned (an event that happened 4-6 years earlier), so some scholars state that Rasulullah's death was actually a result of delayed poisoning, and Allah knows best.

The poisoning occurred after the victory at Khaybaar (over the Jewish tribes). A Jewish woman (in other narrations it is the tribe itself) sent Rasulullahﷺ a leg of lamb that had been poisoned. She thought that if Rasulullahﷺ died it would prove he was a liar, and if he survived it would prove he was a real prophet. After taking two mouthfuls of the meat, Allah made the lamb speak to Rasulullahﷺ and inform him of the poison. Rasulullahﷺ asked the woman what she had done and she confirmed that the meat was poisoned.

There are different reports as to what happened to the Jewish woman afterwards. It is agreed that she was not punished for the attempted poisoning of Rasulullahﷺ, but may have later been executed due to the subsequent death of a Sahaabah who ate from the meat as well, and Allah knows best.

Some Sahaaba noted that the poison left a mark (i.e. blackness) inside the mouth, or on the tongue of the Prophetﷺ. It is also reported that during the time following the poisoning, up until his death, Rasulullahﷺ would occasionally feel ill (the aftereffects of the poisoning), and would undergo wet cupping (i.e. Hijaamah) to relive the symptoms, and Allah knows best.

Bibliography

1. Tafseer Ibn Kathir (Abridged), English translation by Shaykh Safiur-Rahman Al-Mubarakpuri, Darussalam Publishers, 2000

2. Sahih Al-Bukhari, English translation by Dr. Muhammed Muhsin Khan, Islamic University, Al-Medina Al-Munawwara, Kazi Publications, 1986

3. Sahih Muslim, English translation by Abdul Hamid Siddiqi, Shaykh Muhammad Ashraf Publishers, 1990

4. The Qur'aan (English translation), Saheeh International, Almunatada Alislami, Abul Qasim Publishing House, 1997

5. Ar-Raheeq Al-Makhtum (The Sealed Nectar): Biography of the Noble Prophet, Safi-ur-Rahman Al-Mubarakpuri, Islamic University, Al-Madina Al-Munawwara, Dar-us-Salam Publications, 1996

More Products Offered by Ad-Duha!

Ad-Duha is <u>not</u> just a bookstore, we offer complete curriculum packages for use by **homeschoolers or Islamic Schools.**

Our courses contain everything needed to teach in a home or classroom environment including:

- Daily Lesson Manuals
- Full-color, illustrated textbooks (no images of humans/animals)
- Activity filled workbooks
- Audiovisual software (no music or images of humans/animals)
- Enrichment activities for every subject and lesson
- Suggested field trips
- Integrated worksheets to reinforce lesson objectives
- Grading sheets
- Test preparation guides...and much more!

To get **free downloadable samples** of all our books and lesson manuals visit our web site at...

www.ad-duha.org

Made in the USA
Columbia, SC
06 September 2018